The Kingdom Network

The Kingdom Network
A Bible Study

Including
The Jesus Relationship Manual

Dean Drawbaugh
Phyllis Amsley-Drawbaugh

© Copyright 2022 — Dean Drawbaugh, Phyllis Amsley-Drawbaugh

All rights reserved. This book is protected by the copyright laws of the United States of America. This book may not be copied or reprinted for commercial gain or profit. The use of short quotations or occasional page copying for personal use is permitted and encouraged. Permission will be granted upon request. All rights reserved worldwide. Scripture quotations marked KJV are from the King James Version. Scripture quotations marked NKJV are from the New King James Version®. Copyright © 1982 by Thomas Nelson. Used by permission. All rights reserved. Scripture quotations marked NIV are from the Holy Bible, New International Version®, NIV® Copyright ©1973, 1978, 1984, 2011 by Biblica, Inc.® Used by permission. All rights reserved worldwide. Scripture quotations marked NLT are from the Holy Bible, New Living Translation, copyright © 1996, 2004, 2015 by Tyndale House Foundation. Used by permission of Tyndale House Publishers, Inc., Carol Stream, Illinois 60188. All rights reserved.

Drawbaugh Publishing Group
150 Horizon Way
Chambersburg, PA 17201

ISBN 13 TP: 978-1-941746-60-8
ISBN 13 eBook: 978-1-941746-61-5

For Worldwide Distribution, Printed in the USA

1 2 3 4 5 6 7 / 26 25 24 23 22

Acknowledgments

We thank Robert Wolff for pushing us to write this book. For taking his valuable time to answer hundreds of questions. His encouragement and support were invaluable in the writing process.

Mostly we thank God for being patient with us while we came up to speed on His vision and the opportunity to offer this work to His Kingdom Network.

Contents

The Genesis of an Idea ix
Topic One – Invitation 1
Topic Two – Application 5
Topic Three – Expansion 11
Topic Four – Jealousy... 15
Topic Five – Exploration... 19
Topic Six – Choice 23
Topic Seven – Observation 27
Topic Eight – Beware 31
Topic Nine – Attacked 37
Topic Ten – Restored Relationships 41
The Jesus Relationship Manual....................................... 47
Jesus' Parables – Order of Presentation.......................... 49
Conclusion – Revelation of Relationships and Life..... 121

The Genesis of an Idea

One of the Free Dictionary definitions of a "network" is "an association of individuals having a common interest and often providing mutual assistance, information, etc."

Our definition of networking is about building relationships and exchanging ideas in a way that is beneficial to everyone involved. The power is in creating the right relationships with the right people, so that when you need advice you have knowledgeable and trusted people to turn to.

Networking has become a way of life for many professional people. It provides a way to leverage their skills and talents with like-minded people. When a network works right, it creates a wonderful synergy of adding your talent to a pool of knowledge, and at the same time you can extract from it what you need. All involved come out ahead.

Each of us, in one way or another, is part of many networks that can offer support including: family, friends, church, social, media, clubs, neighborhoods, work-related, or children-related activities. The list is almost endless covering every role in your life.

However, have you ever wondered if there a network that will help you prepare to enter the Kingdom of Heaven?

We say, "Yes!" And this Bible study—*The Kingdom Network*—gives you the insights and a biblical foundation for how you get involved and how Heaven is within your reach.

Welcome to The Kingdom Network Bible Study—let's get started!

Topic One

Invitation

For God so loved the world, that He gave His only begotten Son, that whoever believes in Him should not perish but have everlasting life (John 3:16 NKJV).

With one simple verse, God invited everyone to be part of His network. You only need to meet the requirements—believe in Him—to be part of the greatest network the world has ever known. Who wouldn't want to say, "I'm a member in good standing of the Kingdom Network? I am going to Heaven!"

When God sent Jesus to earth to save humankind, He came for everyone. He did not ask about our religious beliefs, our gender, how we look, how we dress, our political views, our financial situation, who we associate with, or our nationality. God sent Jesus to save everyone.

Just as Jesus welcomed everyone into the Kingdom Network when He walked on earth, He extends His invitation to everyone today.

From God's Word in John 10:15-16 (NKJV):

As the Father knows Me, even so I know the Father; and I lay down My life for the sheep. And other sheep I have which are not of this fold; them also I must bring, and they will hear My voice; and there will be one flock and one shepherd.

Jesus willingly died for our sins—He laid down His life for the sheep, which includes people *not of this fold*. He allowed Himself to be nailed to the cross where He suffered and died a painful death to take away our sin—the sins of the world (see Galatians 1:4; 1 John 2:2).

In the Kingdom network, God doesn't ask for anything upfront from us, there are no negotiations and no legal contracts for what we must give in return for Jesus' sacrifice. Neither God nor Jesus ask for any compensation of any kind—the intention is simply and solely to offer salvation to everyone.

Who wouldn't want to be part of the same network as God, Jesus, and the Holy Spirit? We, His children, can talk to God the Father anytime about anything. Prayer is one of the many privileges of the Kingdom Network.

Have you ever had a relationship where so much was given yet so little asked in return?

The Value of a Relationship

Jesus' life on earth was all about relationships. When He was crucified, Jesus only had the clothes on His back. He owned no property, and had no money, no possessions. John 19:23-24 (NIV) tells us:

When the soldiers crucified Jesus, they took his clothes, dividing them into four shares, one for each of them, with the undergarment remaining. This garment was seamless, woven in one piece from top to bottom.

"Let's not tear it," they said to one another. "Let's decide by lot who will get it." This happened that the scripture might be fulfilled that said, "They divided my clothes among them and cast lots for my garment." So this is what the soldiers did.

Jesus had and has the power to have any earthly treasure He wants—wealth, power, and status, to name a few. However, in the end Jesus allowed them to take every possession He had. The only thing Jesus kept and greatly valued was His relationships with His heavenly Father, His earthly family, His friends, and His followers. To Jesus, relationships mattered—possessions did not.

This is the way Jesus lived His life on earth. He freely gave of Himself to everyone He met—from the person with the least possibility of repaying His kindness to the person with the best possibility of repaying His kindness. Jesus was providing us a blueprint on how we should treat people both in this world and in Heaven. In short, Jesus spent His life growing the Kingdom Network.

Points to Ponder

When it is time for you to leave this world, will it be said that you spent your time establishing a network of lasting relationships, or will it be said that you spent your time collecting possessions?

Think of it this way, if we use Jesus' example, you can take the relationships established within the Kingdom Network with you to Heaven. However, the material possessions you have acquired during your life must stay here.

The difference between collecting relationships and collecting possessions is how you build your personal network and where you set your priorities.

Discussion Questions

1. Have you accepted God's invitation to the Kingdom Network?
2. Are your relationships aligned with the Kingdom Network?
3. How wisely do you use your possessions?

TOPIC TWO
Application

Let's look at the invitation again:

For God so loved the world, that He gave His only begotten Son, that whoever believes in Him should not perish but have everlasting life (John 3:16 NKJV).

There are varying interpretations of what John 3:16 means. Everyone seems to agree that God sent Jesus to earth to die for our sins. And most believe that only through our relationship with Jesus will we get to Heaven after our time on earth is completed. The difference in beliefs comes in the phrase *"whoever believes in Him."*

Question 1 – Is it enough to believe Jesus is who He says He is, or do you need to believe in what Jesus believes in? There is such a thing as faith that does not save. The demons believe in God, but aren't saved. From James 2:19

You believe that there is one God. Good! Even the demons believe that—and shudder.

Most people will answer they "need to believe in what Jesus believes in."

Question 2 – If Jesus came today and asked you to stop what you are doing and follow Him, would you stop immediately, no hesitation, and follow Him? Even if it meant living a much different lifestyle?

Most people will answer, "Yes, of course I would do that."

Question 3 - Would you do the same things today on your own without Jesus being next to you and prompting you?

Many would ask, "What would that look like?"

Jesus answers this question in Matthew 25:31-46 (NIV) and explains it well:

"When the Son of Man comes in his glory, and all the angels with him, he will sit on his glorious throne. All the nations will be gathered before him, and he will separate the people one from another as a shepherd separates the sheep from the goats. He will put the sheep on his right and the goats on his left. Then the King will say to those on his right, 'Come, you who are blessed by my Father; take your inheritance, the kingdom prepared for you since the creation of the world. For I was hungry and you gave me something to eat, I was thirsty and you gave me something to drink, I was a stranger and you invited me in, I needed clothes and you clothed me, I was sick and you looked after me, I was in prison and you came to visit me.' Then the righteous will answer him, 'Lord, when did we see you hungry and feed you, or thirsty and give you something to drink? When did we see you a stranger and invite you in, or needing clothes and clothe you? When did we see you sick or in prison and go to visit you?' "The

King will reply, 'Truly I tell you, whatever you did for one of the least of these brothers and sisters of mine, you did for me.'"

For the sheep, us, this is *great* news:

"Then he will say to those on his left, 'Depart from me, you who are cursed, into the eternal fire prepared for the devil and his angels. For I was hungry and you gave me nothing to eat, I was thirsty and you gave me nothing to drink, I was a stranger and you did not invite me in, I needed clothes and you did not clothe me, I was sick and in prison and you did not look after me.' They also will answer, 'Lord, when did we see you hungry or thirsty or a stranger or needing clothes or sick or in prison, and did not help you?' He will reply, 'Truly I tell you, whatever you did not do for one of the least of these, you did not do for me.' Then they will go away to eternal punishment, but the righteous to eternal life."

It's a really *bad* day for the goats!

Either Or

Did you notice there is no third option? You are either a sheep or a goat. This passage of Scripture shows it is not sufficient to sit back, relax, and say, "I believe in Jesus so I'm saved." That's just a good start. While our relationship with Jesus gets us into Heaven, it is our relationship with others that solidifies our relationship with Jesus.

On the Day of Judgment will Jesus ask our religious beliefs, our gender, how we look, how we dress, our political views, our financial situation, who we associated with, or our nationality? Probably not. He already knows! He will simply send the sheep to Heaven and the goats to the eternal fire.

So, in every contact with people, every day whether passing someone on the street you don't know, or greeting your most trusted friend, you can choose to approach that person with a sheep mentality and treat even a stranger as a friend. Or you can choose to approach people with a goat mentality, ignoring their Kingdom needs, and treating even a friend as a stranger.

If you *believe in Him* (Jesus) and how He would have you live your life, one of the most important ways to preserve your standing in the Kingdom Network is to focus on building positive relationships with everyone you come in contact with.

Points to Ponder

Have you noticed that even when you first approach someone, you get an immediate initial impression of that person? We quickly evaluate who that person is by appearance and make value judgments, although with no basis for those judgments. What we choose to do next is a clear indicator of who we are. Are we approaching someone as sheep or goats—remembering what Jesus said in the Scripture passage from Matthew 25? Don't forget, there is no third option.

Changing your approach to people may change your life both before and after death. Are you willing to plant the seeds of who you want to be in every contact and every relationship you have?

Discussion Questions

1. How would you treat Jesus if you met Him today?
2. How do you plan to treat people you meet today?
3. Would you treat Jesus different from the way you treat people now? If yes, explain why.

Topic Three

Expansion

If you have read to this point in the study, you already know four members of the Kingdom Network: God, Jesus, the Holy Spirit, and yourself. It's time to explore the rest of the network and *expand* the list of Kingdom Network people you know.

In your daily spiritual life, you will meet people who believe in Jesus and are members of the Kingdom Network. You will also meet people who don't believe in Jesus and are not members of the Kingdom Network.

Meeting Another Network Member

God creates everyone to be part of the Kingdom Network. And everyone is part of the network at birth. If you want to leave the network, you must choose to commit sin on your own and walk away. It's your choice. You can also truly repent and return to the Network at any time.

When you meet someone who is a member in the Kingdom Network, everything is as God intends it to be—people sharing, providing for, and supporting each other. Wouldn't it be great if everyone acted this way toward one another?

Always strive to know Network people, add them to your Kingdom membership list, and invite them into your personal network.

As an example, let's review the first in-network relationship reflected in the Bible, which happened between God and Adam. From Genesis 1:26-31 (NKJV) we read:

Then God said, "Let Us make man in Our image, according to Our likeness; let them have dominion over the fish of the sea, over the birds of the air, and over the cattle, over all the earth and over every creeping thing that creeps on the earth." So God created man in His own image; in the image of God He created him; male and female He created them. Then God blessed them, and God said to them, "Be fruitful and multiply; fill the earth and subdue it; have dominion over the fish of the sea, over the birds of the air, and over every living thing that moves on the earth." And God said, "See, I have given you every herb that yields seed which is on the face of all the earth, and every tree whose fruit yields seed; to you it shall be for food. Also, to every beast of the earth, to every bird of the air, and to everything that creeps on the earth, in which there is life, I have given every green herb for food"; and it was so. Then God saw everything that He had made, and indeed it was very good. So the evening and the morning were the sixth day.

If you need a definition of someone in the Kingdom Network, or want a picture to put in your mind, look at what God did for Adam. In this short passage we can clearly see that He provided everything Adam needed to live an abundant life.

God is everyone's first relationship. He knew you before you were born and provides everything you need before and after your birth. However, the strength or weakness of this relationship depends on you. God's part is consistent and perfect. If you approach Him as you should, He will share with you what is His, and freely give you what you need.

God has provided everyone with gifts to share. While you may not be able to provide everything someone needs, you should be able to provide something that will help their situation. And that person may have something to help your situation. This is the Kingdom Network in action—both people benefit.

In the remainder of this book we will lean heavily on our relationship with God. Remember, we are all novices in relationships compared to God. He was and is the first relationship for every man and woman who ever lived— billions at last count. Trust in God and let Him take the lead and you will enjoy everything the Kingdom Network has to offer.

Points to Ponder

Members of the Kingdom Network are privileged to study relationships in God's master class— providing us the opportunity to learn from the best. Additionally, to be sure we can handle the teaching, the Holy Spirit is always available to answer questions. John 14:26 (NKJV) tells us: *"But the Helper, the Holy Spirit, whom the Father will send in My name, He will teach you all things, and bring to your remembrance all things that I said to you."* If we then put into practice these lessons, we will have healthy relationships.

Discussion Questions

1. How does the Kingdom Network support your relationships?
2. How do your relationships support the Kingdom Network?
3. How many members of the Kingdom Network do you personally know?

Topic Four
Jealousy

Satan was upset. First, he and his followers were thrown out of Heaven (see Isaiah 14:12-15). Second, he did not receive an invitation to join God's Kingdom network. And finally, the Kingdom Network makes the bond between God and His people stronger, which makes Satan's job harder.

Satan is always jealous of God and what He creates. Whatever God has, Satan wants. As much as God will give you, Satan will take away from you if he can. He is totally focused on himself, all the time.

For an example, let's look at the story of Satan and Eve from Genesis 3:1-8 (NLT):

The serpent was the shrewdest of all the wild animals the Lord God had made. One day he asked the woman, "Did God really say you must not eat the fruit from any of the trees in the garden?" "Of course we may eat fruit from the trees in the garden," the woman replied. It's only the fruit from the tree in the middle of the garden that we are not allowed to eat. God said, 'You must not eat it or even touch it; if you do, you will die.'"

"You won't die!" the serpent replied to the woman. "God knows that your eyes will be opened as soon

> *as you eat it, and you will be like God, knowing both good and evil."*
>
> *The woman was convinced. She saw that the tree was beautiful and its fruit looked delicious, and she wanted the wisdom it would give her. So she took some of the fruit and ate it. Then she gave some to her husband, who was with her, and he ate it, too. At that moment their eyes were opened, and they suddenly felt shame at their nakedness. So they sewed fig leaves together to cover themselves.*
>
> *When the cool evening breezes were blowing, the man and his wife heard the Lord God walking about in the garden. So they hid from the Lord God among the trees.*

Satan knew what was right and what was wrong, and he wanted to break the relationship between God and Adam and Eve. What God had, Satan wanted.

Both Adam and Eve also knew what was right and what was wrong. However, in the end, Satan cleverly put Adam into a position of listening to either Eve or God. Adam listened to Eve, which was the wrong decision. No longer were they happy and at peace, living in the perfect setting with the perfect relationship with their Creator God who created everything.

If Satan could create, we would see evidence of his creations. Satan can't create, he can only attempt to manipulate what God has already created. The only way Satan can increase his followers is to steal them from the Kingdom Network. The Kingdom Network makes Satan's life miserable. When we accept His salvation and become believers, people live as God intended instead of serving Satan. God's people are happy.

To compete with God and steal from the Kingdom Network, Satan tried to steal God's idea and start a similar network. We call Satan's network the "Hell-o Network," which is a play on words to remind you where Satan wants you to end up. Fortunately, Satan had and has a marketing problem. Think how difficult it would be to run a travel agency with Hell as your only destination. This is one of the many stark contrasts between a relationship with God or with Satan—ending up either in Heaven or hell.

But there is a second meaning to the Hell-o Network. Think about it this way. God knows you intimately; He created you. God knows everything about you. God loves you for who you are.

Satan, on the other hand, doesn't know you. But he knows he must try and pull you away from your relationship with God to get what he wants. So Satan must always start with an introduction, saying, "Hell-o!"

Satan's Hell-o

Satan saying hell-o is the first step in his deception The first step into inviting you into his Hell-o Network. Sometimes it is difficult to recognize his introduction as we often don't know who is greeting us.

It is a difficult position to be in. We want to be welcoming and grow God's Kingdom Network, but at the same time we know we must be wary of not being enticed into the Hell-o Network. How can we know the difference and make the right decision?

Remember, only when we place ourselves under God's protection and remain in His Kingdom Network do we have power over Satan. When he realizes who he is dealing with—a protected and committed child of God—then Satan will move on to another person he will try to deceive.

You must be careful when you meet someone you think is not in the Kingdom Network. Satan may be testing the waters—he might be saying hell-o.

Points to Ponder

Just as you know who you are by the way you choose to address people, how people react to you when you first meet someone indicates who they are. Let me give you an example.

First, there are people who *need* help and people who *want* help. Someone with a Kingdom Network mentality will sincerely ask for what you can give and be happy with it. Conversely, people with a Hell-o Network mentality will put their hand out as often as you put something in it, and then ask for more.

Second, as the well-worn saying goes, "You can give someone a fish or teach someone to fish." Many people will take a fish. A Kingdom Network member will be willing to learn to fish to support themselves. A Hell-o Network member will not want to take the time to learn, and will instead look for people to take advantage of.

Discussion Questions

1. How do you recognize someone in the Hell-o Network?
2. Do you know someone(s) in the Hell-o Network?
3. When Satan or one of his minions greets you with, "Hell-o," do you reply, "Hell-o," or "Hell-no"? Why?

Topic Five

Exploration

What happens when you meet someone and you are not sure if the person is in the Kingdom Network or not? What if that person sometimes appears one way and sometime appears another way? Perhaps friendly one moment and conniving the next moment.

Simply, when you first meet someone it is difficult to know who they are and what are their values or motives. How do you know what to do? How do you treat them? Let's consider two stories from the Bible that may offer a solution, to those questions.

Let's review the story of Adam and Eve from Genesis 2:18-25 (NKJV):

Then the Lord And the Lord God said, "It is not good that man should be alone; I will make him a helper comparable to him." Out of the ground the Lord God formed every beast of the field and every bird of the air, and brought them to Adam to see what he would call them. And whatever Adam called each living creature, that was its name. So Adam gave names to all cattle, to the birds of the air, and to every beast of the field. But for Adam there was not found a helper comparable to him. And the Lord God caused a deep sleep to fall on Adam, and he slept; and He took one of his ribs, and closed up the flesh in its place. Then the rib which the Lord God had taken from man He made into a woman, and He brought her to the man. And Adam said: "This is now bone of my bones

And flesh of my flesh; she shall be called Woman, Because she was taken out of Man." Therefore a man shall leave his father and mother and be joined to his wife, and they shall become one flesh. And they were both naked, the man and his wife, and were not ashamed.

At this point in the story Adam and Eve are as close as two people can get, each sharing and caring for the other. Few relationships are closer than a good marriage. But we know that this story doesn't end well (read Genesis 3).

A second story. Reading from chapter 10 of Luke:

And behold, a certain lawyer stood up and tested Him, saying, "Teacher, what shall I do to inherit eternal life?" He said to him, "What is written in the law? What is your reading of it?" So he answered and said, "'You shall love the Lord your God with all your heart, with all your soul, with all your strength, and with all your mind,' and 'your neighbor as yourself.'" And He said to him, "You have answered rightly; do this and you will live." But he, wanting to justify himself, said to Jesus, "And who is my neighbor?"

Then Jesus answered and said: "A certain man went down from Jerusalem to Jericho, and fell among thieves, who stripped him of his clothing, wounded him, and departed, leaving him half dead. Now by chance a certain priest came down that road. And when he saw him, he passed by on the other side. Likewise a Levite, when he arrived at the place, came and looked, and passed by on the other side. But a certain Samaritan, as he journeyed, came where he was. And when he saw him, he had compassion. So he went to him and bandaged his wounds, pouring on oil and wine; and he set him on his own animal, brought him to an inn, and took care of him. On the next day, when he departed, he took out two denarii, gave them to the innkeeper, and said to him, 'Take care of him; and whatever more you spend, when I come again, I will repay you.' So which of these three do you think was neighbor to him who fell among the thieves?"

And he said, "He who showed mercy on him." Then Jesus said to him, "Go and do likewise" (Luke 10:25-37 NKJV).

When you meet someone new there is a settling-in period of time when you learn about the other person. This is when you are not sure if you are talking to a person in the Kingdom Network or the Hell-o Network.

From the first story, there is no set time table to make a decision about trusting a relationship—it can take weeks or months or even years until you are sure. Unfortunately, with Satan in the picture, a relationship can change from good to bad overnight. On the contrary, with God in your corner a relationship can change from bad to good in an instant.

From the second story, we learn that we may meet someone we don't like or don't agree with; however, no matter the person's affliction or affiliation we must still be kind and help the person if possible.

Points to Ponder

We can predict that if two people meet from the Kingdom Network, there is a good chance they will enjoy a healthy relationship. Each person will support the other.

However if one is in the Kingdom Network and the other isn't, there will probably not be a very healthy or mutually beneficial relationship. One will be a giver and the other one a taker.

Discussion Questions

1. Looking at your current relationships, can you determine who are members of the Kingdom Network and those who are not?

2. Of those who are in the Kingdom Network, is it necessary to bridge any gap between their commitment level to your commitment level?

3. What safeguards, if any, do you use when you are not sure if the person you are talking to is in the Kingdom Network?

Topic Six

Choice

You can't follow Jesus while talking with or listening to Satan!

This truth reminds me of the old cartoons of a person trying to make a decision, and there is a devil-like figure on one shoulder and an angel-like figure on the other. Each are pleading their case to the person between them.

Notice the two are never on the same shoulder. They are never pulling in the same direction. They are always at odds.

God and Satan are always in a tug-of-war for your attention, with you in the middle. If you agree with Satan, he will lead you in the wrong direction. Consider, you can't get to your destination if you are going in the wrong direction. So why are you listening?

I read a great statement on a t-shirt the other day: "Be careful who you trust, salt and sugar look the same." The Bible clearly states that God is the only way, truth, and light in life. Satan may twist the truth to sound as if he is for you, but he never is. Appearances can be deceiving like salt and sugar. Therefore, we *must* listen, recognize, and follow only God's voice exclusively.

From Exodus 20:1-7 (NIV) God commands:

And God spoke all these words: "I am the Lord your God, who brought you out of Egypt, out of the land of slavery. You shall have no other gods before me. You shall not make for yourself an image in the form of anything in heaven above or on the earth beneath or in the waters below. You shall not bow down to them or worship them; for I, the Lord your God, am a jealous God, punishing the children for the sin of the parents to the third and fourth generation of those who hate me, but showing love to a thousand generations of those who love me and keep my commandments. You shall not misuse the name of the Lord your God, for the Lord will not hold anyone guiltless who misuses his name.

From Luke 4:5-7 (NIV) we learn that Satan also wants our praise and worship:

The devil led him [Jesus] *up to a high place and showed him in an instant all the kingdoms of the world. And he said to him, "I will give you all their authority and splendor; it has been given to me, and I can give it to anyone I want to. If you worship me, it will all be yours."*

So which is salt and which is sugar?

The difference is in what we receive in return for our worship.

We have already studied that God gave Adam everything he would ever need, and did so until Adam stopped listening to Him and started taking advice from Satan through Eve. God does the same for us when we take His most wise counsel—gives us all we need. Simply, God our Father makes it about us, and what He can do for us, a true Shepherd's mentality. This is who He was, and who He is, and who He will always be.

The Bible lists traits that define Satan:

- He is ruthless: *"Be sober, be vigilant; because your adversary the devil walks about like a roaring lion, seeking whom he may devour"* (1 Peter 5:8 NKJV).

- He is powerful: *"Yet Michael the archangel, in contending with the devil, when he disputed about the body of Moses, dared not bring against him a reviling accusation, but said, "The Lord rebuke you!"* (Jude 1:9 NKJV).

- He is deceitful: *"Put on the whole armor of God, that you may be able to stand against the wiles of the devil. For we do not wrestle against flesh and blood, but against principalities, against powers, against the rulers of the darkness of this age, against spiritual hosts of wickedness in the heavenly places. Therefore take up the whole armor of God, that you may be able to withstand in the evil day, and having done all, to stand"* (Ephesians 6:11-13 NKJV).

- He is crafty: *"But I fear, lest somehow, as the serpent deceived Eve by his craftiness, so your minds may be corrupted from the simplicity that is in Christ. For if he who comes preaches another Jesus whom we have not preached, or if you receive a different spirit which you have not received, or a different gospel which you have not accepted—you may well put up with it!* (2 Corinthians 11:3-4 NKJV).

Do you see the difference between God and Satan? With God the relationship is all about what He can do for us. With Satan it is all about what we should do for him.

God gives freely, so we feel we can also give freely, knowing that God always has more for us. *Satan takes viciously,* so we fear we will never have enough. Therefore we don't give; rather, we hoard what we have.

It's the same with relationships. If you support your relationships, they will flourish; if you take away your support, your relationships will wither and die.

The tug of war for our allegiance continues with God on one shoulder giving to us, and Satan on the other shoulder trying to take away from us.

Points to Ponder

Will you give your allegiance to God or to Satan? At death you will be giving away the excess of what God has provided you. Just as when Jesus died on the cross, He didn't take His possessions with Him to Heaven—neither can you. So will you give to Satan for his pleasure, or support someone in the Kingdom Network who needs it?

Discussion Questions

1. Who are you listening to on a daily basis?
2. Are you getting the best advice?
3. When you write your Kingdom Network last will and testament, who will get your possessions?

Topic Seven

Observation

Satan's Game Plan

God is about pulling everyone together. As the Good Shepherd with His flock, God wants to pull us together so He can love us and protect us and keep us on the right path. Even to the extent of seeing the importance of one lost lamb. From Luke 15:3-7 (NIV):

> *Then Jesus told them this parable: "Suppose one of you has a hundred sheep and loses one of them. Doesn't he leave the ninety-nine in the open country and go after the lost sheep until he finds it? And when he finds it, he joyfully puts it on his shoulders and goes home. Then he calls his friends and neighbors together and says, 'Rejoice with me; I have found my lost sheep.' I tell you that in the same way there will be more rejoicing in heaven over one sinner who repents than over ninety-nine righteous persons who do not need to repent.*

Have you ever asked yourself who separated the single sheep from the flock?

Satan is looking to separate us from God's flock so he can steal souls one at a time; the classic divide and conquer strategy. Have you noticed in our short examples, in this book, that Satan:

1. Waited for Eve to be alone to deceive her
2. Waited for Jesus to be by Himself in the wilderness before trying to deceive Him

Simply, it is easier to sell a deception to a smaller group of people rather than a large group. When there are more people in a group—such as the Kingdom Network—there is a better chance that someone will notice the con game and expose it for what it is. So Satan attacks the single lamb instead of the flock.

Satan is a master at separating people from each other. He does it ever so subtly that over time we don't even recognize it is happening, or has already happened.

Consider when humankind labels groups of people, it is really Satan segmenting the Kingdom Network so it can be attacked easily. Smaller groups play into Satan's game plan.

Do you recognize these Satan-instigated separations and labels that our society regularly use against each other?

- Nationality
- Gender
- Sexual preference
- Ethnicity
- Religion
- Political views
- Health
- Wealth

- Appearance
- Weight
- Education
- Skin Color
- Friends and acquaintances
- Family
- Age
- Occupation
- Affiliations
- On and on goes the list

Each of these aspects of life can divide the population as a whole into smaller and smaller groups. The smaller the whole becomes, the easier it is for Satan to attack. (For instance, a middle-aged business person, financially strapped, and in questionable health.)

Satan's game plan is to force us into a small box so it is easier to manipulate us. Satan would like us to focus on people's differences, however small, because this breaks us into groups that he can better attack. When Christians are all part of the Kingdom Network, we will be a powerful group who can withstand the devil's plans.

Point to Ponder

So, God is looking for relations, the closer the better. And Satan is looking for separations, the farther the better. What traits do you use to evaluate a person on a first impression basis? Are you using your first impressions to support people (relations) or to judge people (separations)?

Discussion Questions

1. What label(s) from the list are you uncomfortable being associated with?
2. Why does being linked to this label concern you?
3. Do you feel Satan can attack you using this label?

Topic Eight

Beware

Satan's Toolbox

Satan is a salesperson by nature. I picture him as a snake oil salesman or an obnoxious telemarketer. He gets nowhere until you buy in to what he is selling that day. He will use any tactic, no matter how underhanded, to get the sale. He is looking for your weakness and will pounce on it without hesitation.

Once Satan knows your weakness, he only needs to wait for the right timing. You will not hear Satan's voice, you will not see a large billboard with flashing lights announcing his presence. It will be more subtle, such as you may start to notice "negative thoughts" creeping into you mind.

From Luke 22:31-34 (NIV) Jesus says:

"Simon, Simon, Satan has asked to sift all of you as wheat. But I have prayed for you, Simon, that your faith may not fail. And when you have turned back, strengthen your brothers." But he replied, "Lord, I am ready to go with you to prison and to death." Jesus answered, "I tell you, Peter, before the rooster crows

today, you will deny three times that you know me."

Later in Luke 22:54-60 (NIV) we read:

Then seizing him [Jesus], they led him away and took him into the house of the high priest. Peter followed at a distance. And when some there had kindled a fire in the middle of the courtyard and had sat down together, Peter sat down with them. A servant girl saw him seated there in the firelight. She looked closely at him and said, "This man was with him." But he denied it. "Woman, I don't know him," he said. A little later someone else saw him and said, "You also are one of them." "Man, I am not!" Peter replied. About an hour later another asserted, "Certainly this fellow was with him, for he is a Galilean." Peter replied, "Man, I don't know what you're talking about!" Just as he was speaking, the rooster crowed.

In these Scripture passages we see that Satan waited to attack Simon until he was away from his network and unsupported. Simon's weakness was fear. So Satan used Simon's fear against him, the fear of being arrested.

Satan looks for separation, then waits until you are alone, waits until you have no support, waits until you think he is the only one talking. Using what separates you from others, Satan tells you what a bad situation you're in. He uses your negative emotions to drive his point home. He uses your feelings against you.

Feelings aren't necessarily facts. Feelings are usually short-term beliefs that change as the situation changes. Satan wants you to react to partial information. Satan puts into your mind the feeling that you have been given the short end of the stick.

You might hear your inner voice say:

- Doesn't that make you nervous? How will you survive? (Anxieties)
- He has it in for you, don't trust anything he says. (Authority)
- If she did that to me, I would be very upset (Anger)
- Nobody is going through what you are. You are way out on the limb, all by yourself. (Loneliness)
- If you could only do this/that it would show them (Deal-making)
- Aren't you afraid of what they will do to you next? (Fear)
- I can see why you are ready to give up, I would be too. (Depression)
- You don't have a chance doing it their way (Reality)
- You might as well accept your position, it won't get any better. (Acceptance)
- Wouldn't you like to get even? (Temptation)

Did you ever catch yourself thinking this way? Did it create stress in your life? Those thoughts were *not* from God. That voice was *not* God's voice, which is the voice of peace and love—*not stress or anxiety, not condemnation or shame, not anger or fear.*

Stress is sometimes defined as the difference between who you are and who you want to be. Satan often works in this gray area, this area that causes stress. His goal is to control you or get you far enough into the stress area that he can attack you or use you to attack someone else.

However in the Kingdom Network, we know God will provide all we need, which does *not* include stress.

Philippians 4:19 (NKJV) tells us, *"And my **God shall supply all your needs** according to His riches in glory by Christ Jesus."* Satan wants you to forget that promise from God. Satan wants you to feel you have been forgotten. When you agree with the evil one, he offers you his solution, which is doom and gloom and destruction. Satan wants you to think he is the only one on your shoulder giving good advice. Don't listen to him—flee!

> *Submit yourselves, then, to God. Resist the devil, and he will flee from you* (James 4:7 NIV).

Points to Ponder

Review the following characteristics. Do any make you feel uncomfortable with who you are?

- Nationality
- Gender
- Sexual preference
- Religion
- Political views
- Health
- Wealth
- Appearance
- Weight
- Education
- Skin Color

- Friends and acquaintances
- Family
- Age
- Occupation
- The list goes on and on

Discussion Questions

1. Which characteristic(s) do you hide from others?
2. Do you believe this trait makes you less of a person in other people's minds?
3. Can Satan use this insecurity to attack you?

Topic Nine

Attacked

A successful attack by Satan against a member of the Kingdom Network can have a ripple effect on many others. As you read the following case study, count the number of people directly affected by this attack. Then imagine the number of people they come in contact with. And the number of people they come in contact with. And so on.

A Case Study

Joe and one of his close friends have an ongoing discussion on politics. They aren't in agreement; consequently, they are always looking for new ammunition to convince the other of their point of view. Several weeks ago Joe noticed a news article that gave him the information he thought he needed. He could hardly wait until they met that night to unveil his evidence.

A few hours later Joe was driving home with what seemed to be the weight of the world on his shoulders. He had just left the gathering where he had lost his temper, lost the argument, and possibly lost one of his best friends.

Now, several weeks later, he still had that conversation on his mind. It kept creeping into his thoughts. No matter how he tried to do other things, he couldn't avoid thinking about his friend and their unfortunate conversation. He wasn't sleeping, he was tense at work, it was straining other relationships, and he was confrontational with people he didn't even know. The stress of this strained relationship was causing a downward spiral. Joe was at a crossroad.

This circumstance doesn't have to involve politics, it can be any contentious discussion. But as you can see Satan is not only attacking Joe, others in his Kingdom Network were being effected. Joe's family, friends, associates, and people he doesn't even know are on the receiving end of Joe's frustration. Sadly, Joe may be helping Satan set up others for a similar attack.

From Philippians 4:6-9 (NLT):

Don't worry about anything; instead, pray about everything. Tell God what you need, and thank him for all he has done. Then you will experience God's peace, which exceeds anything we can understand. His peace will guard your hearts and minds as you live in Christ Jesus. And now, dear brothers and sisters, one final thing. Fix your thoughts on what is true, and honorable, and right, and pure, and lovely, and admirable. Think about things that are excellent and worthy of praise. Keep putting into practice all you learned and received from me—everything you heard from me and saw me doing. Then the God of peace will be with you.

Does this case study sound familiar, have you ever found yourself in a situation similar to what Joe experienced? I know people who are trying to manage several such relationships right now. While one makes you unproductive in other roles of your life, several may render you completely ineffective. And Satan wins!

Relationships that aren't healthy rob you of time that could be used elsewhere to a better advantage. When you mend broken relationships, a more successful life is within your grasp.

Not all relationships under stress are life altering. However, if you look at the areas of your life that are somewhat out of control, you will notice that most often the root cause of the problem is a relationship with someone.

If you can identify and fix shaky relationships, the effort will go a long way toward repairing your other problem(s) as well. Conversely, if you don't fix the relationship, it will stall your progress or get you off track in other areas of your life, snowballing into a possible major conflict.

Points to Ponder

Relationships that are headed in the wrong direction are attacks on you and the Kingdom Network by Satan. It is imperative to repair them as quickly as possible to keep you in good standing and the Network strong to defend against future attacks.

Are there areas in your life that are not going as smoothly as you would like? Areas where you would like to be moving forward but find a roadblock followed by a roadblock followed by another roadblock?

Take the time to list them now, if possible. Be specific and detailed about what is happening. Then try to associate a relationship or person who might be holding you back.

Discussion Questions

1. How many of your relationships are stalled or off track?
2. How much time and effort are you investing on these relationships?
3. How would your life improve if you could resolve your relationship issues?

Topic Ten

Restored Relationships

Brothers and sisters, if someone is caught in a sin, you who live by the Spirit should restore that person gently. But watch yourselves, or you also may be tempted (Galatians 6:1 NIV).

Introduction to the Jesus Relationship Manual

Strained relationships diminish other activities in our life, and as a result the quality of our life. It is therefore prudent to resolve relationship issues as quickly as possible and to try to prevent them in the first place. In this way we lessen the attack on the Kingdom Network.

You may have picked up this book seeing *The Jesus Relationship Manual* on the front cover and thought, *Jesus didn't write a relationship manual!* And you would be right. But give us a bit of latitude here.

When reading Jesus teaching the parables to the people in the Gospels, you can't help but notice that they are chocked full of relationship advice. While He did not write them down in manual form, His speaking is like a relationship podcast of our time. Except, of course, His words were full of godly truth and wisdom well beyond any of today's broadcasts.

Question—how many times have you paused when reading a Bible verse and thought, *My friend should read this!* knowing that the information would make a difference in what your friend is currently experiencing in life.

Jesus' parables offer the solution to many of your own personal relationship problems as well. What is needed is an effective way to organize and cross reference the information so you can get to it when needed. The remainder of this book does just that. Steps are provided to recognize and then use the power and wisdom in the parables.

For You

Select an area of your life that could be improved and the person you feel is the road block in having a healthy relationship. You need to collect two other pieces of information before we turn to the parables.

First, what are you feeling? Often what you are feeling is what is happening. Are you feeling happy, are you feeling angry, are you feeling cheated? How you feel is a good indicator of the current health of the relationship.

Second, how do you think the other person is feeling? The other person's feelings are just as important as yours, but harder to gauge. Is your last conversation on his or her mind as well? Does the person feel disappointed, defeated, discouraged, intimidated, or guilty?

Now, match these two emotions to a parable or parables to seek Jesus' advice. It's usually not what is happening as much as the emotion attached to it. We suggest a four-step process:

1. Read through
2. Pray through
3. Follow through
4. For a better life for you!

Read Through

When reading through the parables in the next section, start by identifying every person and every situation mentioned in the parable. And what emotion they are causing at the time?

Are there two characters similar to you and the other person in your troubled relationship? Are there similar situations? If so, mark it down to use in the praying-through section. If not, move to the next parable. You may find several parables that fit your situation. It may take a bit of rewriting to make it fit your situation. The extra effort will bring you extra comfort and resolution.

As an example, let's look at the parable of the lost sheep.

> *"What do you think? If a man owns a hundred sheep, and one of them wanders away, will he not leave the ninety-nine on the hills and go to look for the one that wandered off? And if he finds it, truly I tell you, he is happier about that one sheep than about the ninety-nine that did not wander off. In the same way your Father in heaven is not willing that any of these little ones should perish"* (Matthew 18:12-14 NIV).

Now let's change the word "sheep" to "friend" and consider the parable again:

> *What do you think? If you had a hundred friends, and one of them became upset and left, would you not leave the ninety-nine, and find and comfort that friend who had left?*

Ask yourself: Is my action in line with what the parable is trying to teach? Or should I modify what I am doing?

Ask and answer: If I changed my approach to people in this way, what could I expect to happen?

Pray Through

Praying by itself works, a conversation with God is always a good beginning. And you may need to ask for forgiveness before continuing the rest of the process. Remember, your relationship with God is vital in every relationship in the Kingdom Network.

So, prayer is good and works—but focused prayer is better. If you don't know what you want, how can you ask for help with it?

During your prayer, put forward each of the parables you identified in the reading through step, and how you think they apply to your relationship. You may find that God will fill in what is missing.

Remember, when praying, talking is important—but listening gets you the answers you need.

Follow Through

Following through on your plan to repair a relationship may be the trickiest step of this process. You know what you would like to do. And if you are listening, you know what God wants you to do. But you don't know what the person you are trying to reconcile with is thinking.

As in the parable of the Prodigal Son (see Luke 15:11-32), the father tries to reason with his son. But when that doesn't work, he then waits for his son to be ready to listen.

Sometimes you need to do what you can and then wait for the other person to be ready to receive your approach to the situation. The secret is to make sure you do everything you can to be at peace with the relationship until you're both ready to move forward.

Once you know what to do, you need to act. A few thoughts on action:

- The time to act is when you notice the problem, why wait until you both dig in your heels.
- A journey starts with a single step. If you don't start, you can't reach your destination.
- If you are going in the wrong direction, you will have a long journey at best.

A Better Life for You!

If you didn't need to live in the past and fix relationship after relationship. How much time would you have to do other things? Do you know people who are comfortable with who they are? Do they seem happier than you? Reading, understanding, and applying the wisdom that the parables offer can help you clean up your past and present relationships, and put you in a position for a happier and more productive future.

Discussion Questions and Actions

- Are you willing to and prepared to fix your broken relationships?
- When are you going to get started?
- Whose is the first relationship you need to work on?
- How do you feel?
- How does the other person feel?
- Read through the parables.
- Pray through the selected parables.
- Follow through with the other person.
- Enjoy a better relationship and a healthier you!

The Jesus Relationship Manual
Parables and Select Scripture Readings

Parables are stories with lessons woven into them. Jesus' parables are timeless with many lesson to learn.

We have selected 52 parables and select Scripture readings as vital components to this book on networking for God's Kingdom advancement. We urge you to read through all the parables with the four steps in mind. Then we challenge you to go back and spend one week reading and praying and acting on each one parable separately to fully understand the meaning—and ultimately restore every relationship in your life and expand your Kingdom Network. One parable every week for 52 weeks equals a year of growing and enjoying a more intimate relationship with Jesus.

The parables have been taken from various versions of the Bible, God's Word. Please feel free to use your favorite Bible translation for cross reference and deeper revelation. To save room and to give you space to write in this section, if a parable is cited in more than one book of the Bible, we have printed only the first listed version, and have noted the other references for your convenience.

We have compiled what we believe to be a complete list of Jesus' parables and have included some select Scripture readings that complement them. When reading, you may think of another passage of Scripture that you feel applies, please add it to your list. The more you read God's Word, the more you will understand all types of relationships and how spiritually interconnected we really all are.

Jesus' Parables
Order of Presentation

1. Ability 53
2. A Foul Mouth..55
3. Cost of Discipleship..56
4. Evil Tenants 57
5. Faithful vs. Wicked Servant......................................59
6. Fig Tree 60
7. Friend at Midnight..61
8. Friend in Need 62
9. Friends of the Bridegroom..63
10. Good Samaritan 64
11. Good Shepherd 66
12. Growing Seed 67
13. Hidden Treasure..68
14. Lamp under a Basket..69
15. Lost Coin 70
16. Lost Sheep 71
17. Lowest Seat at the Feast...72
18. Master and Servant...74

19. Money Lender 75
20. Mustard Seed 76
21. Net of Good and Bad Fish 77
22. New Cloth on an Old Garment 78
23. New Wine in Old Wineskins 79
24. Owner of a House 80
25. Persistent Widow 81
26. Pharisee and the Tax Collector 82
27. Prodigal Son 83
28. Rich Fool 86
29. Rich Man and Lazarus 87
30. Savor of Salt 89
31. Sheep and Goats 90
32. Shrewd Manager 92
33. Sower and the Seeds 94
34. Speck and the Log 96
35. Strong Man Armed 97
36. Ten Bridesmaids 98
37. Ten Servants 100
38. The Invitation 102
39. Tree and its Fruit 103
40. Two Sons 104
41. Unclean Spirit 105
42. Unfruitful Fig Tree 106
43. Unmerciful Servant 107

44. Valuable Pearl 109
45. Vine and the Branches 110
46. Vineyard Workers 111
47. Watchful Homeowner...113
48. Watchful Servants 114
49. Wedding Banquet..115
50. Weeds in the Field 117
51. Wise and Foolish Builders......................................119
52. Yeast...120

1
Ability

Matthew 25:14-30 (NIV): *"Again, it will be like a man going on a journey, who called his servants and entrusted his wealth to them. To one he gave five bags of gold, to another two bags, and to another one bag, each according to his ability. Then he went on his journey. The man who had received five bags of gold went at once and put his money to work and gained five bags more. So also, the one with two bags of gold gained two more. But the man who had received one bag went off, dug a hole in the ground and hid his master's money. After a long time the master of those servants returned and settled accounts with them. The man who had received five bags of gold brought the other five. 'Master,' he said, 'you entrusted me with five bags of gold. See, I have gained five more.' His master replied, 'Well done, good and faithful servant! You have been faithful with a few things; I will put you in charge of many things. Come and share your master's happiness!' The man with two bags of gold also came. 'Master,' he said, 'you entrusted me with two bags of gold; see, I have gained two more.'*

"*His master replied, 'Well done, good and faithful servant! You have been faithful with a few things; I will put you in charge of many things. Come and share your master's happiness!' Then the man who had received one bag of gold came. 'Master,' he said, 'I knew that you are a hard man, harvesting where you have not sown and gathering where you have not scattered seed. So I was afraid and went out and hid your gold in the ground. See, here is what belongs to you.' His master replied, 'You wicked, lazy servant! So you knew that I harvest where I have not sown and gather where I have not scattered seed? Well then, you should have put my money on deposit with the bankers, so that when I returned I would have received it back with interest. 'So take the bag of gold from him and give it to the one who has ten bags. For whoever has will be given more, and they will have an abundance. Whoever does not have, even what they have will be taken from them. And throw that worthless servant outside, into the darkness, where there will be weeping and gnashing of teeth.'"* (See also Luke 19:12-27.)

_____

_____

_____

_____

_____

_____

2
A Foul Mouth

Matthew 15:10-14 (NLT): *Then Jesus called to the crowd to come and hear. "Listen," he said, "and try to understand. It's not what goes into your mouth that defiles you; you are defiled by the words that come out of your mouth." Then the disciples came to him and asked, "Do you realize you offended the Pharisees by what you just said?" Jesus replied, "Every plant not planted by my heavenly Father will be uprooted, so ignore them. They are blind guides leading the blind, and if one blind person guides another, they will both fall into a ditch."*

_____

_____

_____

_____

_____

3
Cost of Discipleship

Luke 14:28-33 (NKJV): *"For which of you, intending to build a tower, does not sit down first and count the cost, whether he has enough to finish it—lest, after he has laid the foundation, and is not able to finish, all who see it begin to mock him, saying, 'This man began to build and was not able to finish'? Or what king, going to make war against another king, does not sit down first and consider whether he is able with ten thousand to meet him who comes against him with twenty thousand? Or else, while the other is still a great way off, he sends a delegation and asks conditions of peace. So likewise, whoever of you does not forsake all that he has cannot be My disciple."*

_____

_____

_____

_____

4

Evil Tenants

Matthew 21:33-44 (NIV): *"Listen to another parable: There was a landowner who planted a vineyard. He put a wall around it, dug a winepress in it and built a watchtower. Then he rented the vineyard to some farmers and moved to another place. When the harvest time approached, he sent his servants to the tenants to collect his fruit. The tenants seized his servants; they beat one, killed another, and stoned a third. Then he sent other servants to them, more than the first time, and the tenants treated them the same way. Last of all, he sent his son to them. 'They will respect my son,' he said. "But when the tenants saw the son, they said to each other, 'This is the heir. Come, let's kill him and take his inheritance.' So they took him and threw him out of the vineyard and killed him. Therefore, when the owner of the vineyard comes, what will he do to those tenants? "He will bring those wretches to a wretched end," they replied, "and he will rent the vineyard to other tenants, who will give him his share of the crop at harvest time."*

Jesus said to them, "Have you never read in the Scriptures: "'The stone the builders rejected has become the cornerstone; the Lord has done this, and it is marvelous in our eyes'? Therefore I tell you that the kingdom of God will be taken away from you and given to a people who will produce its fruit. Anyone who falls on this stone will be broken to pieces; anyone on whom it falls will be crushed." (See also Mark 12:1-11; Luke 20:9-18.)

5
Faithful vs. Wicked Servant

Matthew 24:45-51 (NIV): *"Who then is the faithful and wise servant, whom the master has put in charge of the servants in his household to give them their food at the proper time? It will be good for that servant whose master finds him doing so when he returns. Truly I tell you, he will put him in charge of all his possessions. But suppose that servant is wicked and says to himself, 'My master is staying away a long time,' and he then begins to beat his fellow servants and to eat and drink with drunkards. The master of that servant will come on a day when he does not expect him and at an hour he is not aware of. He will cut him to pieces and assign him a place with the hypocrites, where there will be weeping and gnashing of teeth."* (See also Luke 12:42-48.)

_____

_____

_____

_____

6
Fig Tree

Matthew 24:32-35 (NKJV): *"Now learn this parable from the fig tree: When its branch has already become tender and puts forth leaves, you know that summer is near. So you also, when you see all these things, know that it is near—at the doors! Assuredly, I say to you, this generation will by no means pass away till all these things take place. Heaven and earth will pass away, but My words will by no means pass away."* (See also Mark 13:28-31; Luke 21:29-33)

_____

_____

_____

_____

_____

_____

7
Friend at Midnight

Luke 12:3-9 (NLT): *"Whatever you have said in the dark will be heard in the light, and what you have whispered behind closed doors will be shouted from the housetops for all to hear! Dear friends, don't be afraid of those who want to kill your body; they cannot do any more to you after that. But I'll tell you whom to fear. Fear God, who has the power to kill you and then throw you into hell. Yes, he's the one to fear. What is the price of five sparrows—two copper coins? Yet God does not forget a single one of them. And the very hairs on your head are all numbered. So don't be afraid; you are more valuable to God than a whole flock of sparrows. I tell you the truth, everyone who acknowledges me publicly here on earth, the Son of Man will also acknowledge in the presence of God's angels. But anyone who denies me here on earth will be denied before God's angels."*

_____

_____

_____

8

Friend in Need

Luke 11:5-8 (NIV): *Then Jesus said to them, "Suppose you have a friend, and you go to him at midnight and say, 'Friend, lend me three loaves of bread; a friend of mine on a journey has come to me, and I have no food to offer him.' And suppose the one inside answers, 'Don't bother me. The door is already locked, and my children and I are in bed. I can't get up and give you anything.' I tell you, even though he will not get up and give you the bread because of friendship, yet because of your shameless audacity he will surely get up and give you as much as you need."*

9

Friends of the Bridegroom

Matthew 9:15 (NKJV): *"And Jesus said to them, 'Can the friends of the bridegroom mourn as long as the bridegroom is with them? But the days will come when the bridegroom will be taken away from them, and then they will fast.'"* (See also Luke 5:34-35.)

10

Good Samaritan

Luke 10:30-37 (NKJV): *Then Jesus answered and said: "A certain man went down from Jerusalem to Jericho, and fell among thieves, who stripped him of his clothing, wounded him, and departed, leaving him half dead. Now by chance a certain priest came down that road. And when he saw him, he passed by on the other side. Likewise a Levite, when he arrived at the place, came and looked, and passed by on the other side. But a certain Samaritan, as he journeyed, came where he was. And when he saw him, he had compassion. So he went to him and bandaged his wounds, pouring on oil and wine; and he set him on his own animal, brought him to an inn, and took care of him. On the next day, when he departed, he took out two denarii, gave them to the innkeeper, and said to him, 'Take care of him; and whatever more you spend, when I come again, I will repay you.' So which of these three do you think was neighbor to him who fell among the thieves?" And he said, "He who showed mercy on him." Then Jesus said to him, "Go and do likewise."*

11

Good Shepherd

John 10:1-5 (NLT): *"I tell you the truth, anyone who sneaks over the wall of a sheepfold, rather than going through the gate, must surely be a thief and a robber! But the one who enters through the gate is the shepherd of the sheep. The gatekeeper opens the gate for him, and the sheep recognize his voice and come to him. He calls his own sheep by name and leads them out. After he has gathered his own flock, he walks ahead of them, and they follow him because they know his voice. They won't follow a stranger; they will run from him because they don't know his voice."*

_____

_____

_____

_____

_____

12

Growing Seed

Mark 4:26-29 (NKJV): *And He said, "The kingdom of God is as if a man should scatter seed on the ground, and should sleep by night and rise by day, and the seed should sprout and grow, he himself does not know how. For the earth yields crops by itself: first the blade, then the head, after that the full grain in the head. But when the grain ripens, immediately he puts in the sickle, because the harvest has come."*

13

Hidden Treasure

Matthew 13:44 (NLT): *"The Kingdom of Heaven is like a treasure that a man discovered hidden in a field. In his excitement, he hid it again and sold everything he owned to get enough money to buy the field."*

14

Lamp under a Basket

Matthew 5:14-16 (NLT): *"You are the light of the world—like a city on a hilltop that cannot be hidden. No one lights a lamp and then puts it under a basket. Instead, a lamp is placed on a stand, where it gives light to everyone in the house. In the same way, let your good deeds shine out for all to see, so that everyone will praise your heavenly Father."* (See also Mark 4:21-22; Luke 8:16-17, 11:33-36.)

15

Lost Coin

Luke 15:8-10 (NLT): *"Or suppose a woman has ten silver coins and loses one. Won't she light a lamp and sweep the entire house and search carefully until she finds it? And when she finds it, she will call in her friends and neighbors and say, 'Rejoice with me because I have found my lost coin.' In the same way, there is joy in the presence of God's angels when even one sinner repents."*

16

Lost Sheep

Matthew 18:12-14 (NKJV): *"What do you think? If a man owns a hundred sheep, and one of them wanders away, will he not leave the ninety-nine on the hills and go to look for the one that wandered off? And if he finds it, truly I tell you, he is happier about that one sheep than about the ninety-nine that did not wander off. In the same way your Father in heaven is not willing that any of these little ones should perish.* (See also Luke 15:4-7.)

_____

_____

_____

_____

_____

_____

17

Lowest Seat at the Feast

Luke 14:7-14 (NIV): *When he noticed how the guests picked the places of honor at the table, he told them this parable: "When someone invites you to a wedding feast, do not take the place of honor, for a person more distinguished than you may have been invited. If so, the host who invited both of you will come and say to you, 'Give this person your seat.' Then, humiliated, you will have to take the least important place. But when you are invited, take the lowest place, so that when your host comes, he will say to you, 'Friend, move up to a better place.' Then you will be honored in the presence of all the other guests. For all those who exalt themselves will be humbled, and those who humble themselves will be exalted." Then Jesus said to his host, "When you give a luncheon or dinner, do not invite your friends, your brothers or sisters, your relatives, or your rich neighbors; if you do, they may invite you back and so you will be repaid. But when you give a banquet, invite the poor, the crippled, the lame, the blind, and you will be blessed. Although they cannot repay you, you will be repaid at the resurrection of the righteous."*

18

Master and Servant

Luke 17:7-10 (NIV): *"Suppose one of you has a servant plowing or looking after the sheep. Will he say to the servant when he comes in from the field, 'Come along now and sit down to eat'? Won't he rather say, 'Prepare my supper, get yourself ready and wait on me while I eat and drink; after that you may eat and drink'? Will he thank the servant because he did what he was told to do? So you also, when you have done everything you were told to do, should say, 'We are unworthy servants; we have only done our duty.'"*

19

Money Lender

Luke 7:41-43 (NKJV): *"There was a certain creditor who had two debtors. One owed five hundred denarii, and the other fifty. And when they had nothing with which to repay, he freely forgave them both. Tell Me, therefore, which of them will love him more?" Simon answered and said, "I suppose the one whom he forgave more." And He said to him, "You have rightly judged."*

20

Mustard Seed

Matthew 13:31-32 (NKJV): *Another parable He put forth to them, saying: "The kingdom of heaven is like a mustard seed, which a man took and sowed in his field, which indeed is the least of all the seeds; but when it is grown it is greater than the herbs and becomes a tree, so that the birds of the air come and nest in its branches."* (See also Mark 4:30-32; Luke 13:18-19.)

_____

_____

_____

_____

_____

_____

_____

21

Net of Good and Bad Fish

Matthew 13:47-50 (NKJV): *"Again, the kingdom of heaven is like a dragnet that was cast into the sea and gathered some of every kind, which, when it was full, they drew to shore; and they sat down and gathered the good into vessels, but threw the bad away. So it will be at the end of the age. The angels will come forth, separate the wicked from among the just, and cast them into the furnace of fire. There will be wailing and gnashing of teeth."*

22

New Cloth on an Old Garment

Matthew 9:16 (NLT): *"Besides, who would patch old clothing with new cloth? For the new patch would shrink and rip away from the old cloth, leaving an even bigger tear than before."* (See also Mark 2:21; Luke 5:36.)

23

New Wine in Old Wineskins

Matthew 9:17 (NLT): *"And no one puts new wine into old wineskins. For the old skins would burst from the pressure, spilling the wine and ruining the skins. New wine is stored in new wineskins so that both are preserved."* (See also Mark 2:22; Luke 5:37-38.)

_____

_____

_____

_____

_____

_____

_____

_____

24

Owner of a House

Matthew 13:52 (NIV): *He said to them, "Therefore every teacher of the law who has become a disciple in the kingdom of heaven is like the owner of a house who brings out of his storeroom new treasures as well as old."*

25

Persistent Widow

Luke 18:2-8 (NIV): *He said: "In a certain town there was a judge who neither feared God nor cared what people thought. And there was a widow in that town who kept coming to him with the plea, 'Grant me justice against my adversary.' For some time he refused. But finally he said to himself, 'Even though I don't fear God or care what people think, yet because this widow keeps bothering me, I will see that she gets justice, so that she won't eventually come and attack me!'" And the Lord said, "Listen to what the unjust judge says. And will not God bring about justice for his chosen ones, who cry out to him day and night? Will he keep putting them off? I tell you, he will see that they get justice, and quickly. However, when the Son of Man comes, will he find faith on the earth?"*

_____

_____

_____

26
Pharisee and the Tax Collector

Luke 18:9-14 (NIV)*: To some who were confident of their own righteousness and looked down on everyone else, Jesus told this parable: "Two men went up to the temple to pray, one a Pharisee and the other a tax collector. The Pharisee stood by himself and prayed: 'God, I thank you that I am not like other people—robbers, evildoers, adulterers—or even like this tax collector. I fast twice a week and give a tenth of all I get.' But the tax collector stood at a distance. He would not even look up to heaven, but beat his breast and said, 'God, have mercy on me, a sinner.' I tell you that this man, rather than the other, went home justified before God. For all those who exalt themselves will be humbled, and those who humble themselves will be exalted."*

27
Prodigal Son

Luke 15:11-32 (NKJV): *Then He said: "A certain man had two sons. And the younger of them said to his father, 'Father, give me the portion of goods that falls to me.' So he divided to them his livelihood. And not many days after, the younger son gathered all together, journeyed to a far country, and there wasted his possessions with prodigal living. But when he had spent all, there arose a severe famine in that land, and he began to be in want. Then he went and joined himself to a citizen of that country, and he sent him into his fields to feed swine. And he would gladly have filled his stomach with the pods that the swine ate, and no one gave him anything.*

"But when he came to himself, he said, 'How many of my father's hired servants have bread enough and to spare, and I perish with hunger! I will arise and go to my father, and will say to him, "Father, I have sinned against heaven and before you, and I am no longer worthy to be called your son. Make me like one of your hired servants."'

"And he arose and came to his father. But when he was still a great way off, his father saw him and had

compassion, and ran and fell on his neck and kissed him. And the son said to him, 'Father, I have sinned against heaven and in your sight, and am no longer worthy to be called your son.'

"But the father said to his servants, 'Bring out the best robe and put it on him, and put a ring on his hand and sandals on his feet. And bring the fatted calf here and kill it, and let us eat and be merry; for this my son was dead and is alive again; he was lost and is found.' And they began to be merry.

"Now his older son was in the field. And as he came and drew near to the house, he heard music and dancing. So he called one of the servants and asked what these things meant. And he said to him, 'Your brother has come, and because he has received him safe and sound, your father has killed the fatted calf.'

"But he was angry and would not go in. Therefore his father came out and pleaded with him. So he answered and said to his father, 'Lo, these many years I have been serving you; I never transgressed your commandment at any time; and yet you never gave me a young goat, that I might make merry with my friends. But as soon as this son of yours came, who has devoured your livelihood with harlots, you killed the fatted calf for him.'

"And he said to him, 'Son, you are always with me, and all that I have is yours. It was right that we should make merry and be glad, for your brother was dead and is alive again, and was lost and is found.'"

28

Rich Fool

Luke 12:16-21 (NIV): *And he told them this parable: "The ground of a certain rich man yielded an abundant harvest. He thought to himself, 'What shall I do? I have no place to store my crops.' Then he said, 'This is what I'll do. I will tear down my barns and build bigger ones, and there I will store my surplus grain. And I'll say to myself, "You have plenty of grain laid up for many years. Take life easy; eat, drink and be merry."' But God said to him, 'You fool! This very night your life will be demanded from you. Then who will get what you have prepared for yourself?' This is how it will be with whoever stores up things for themselves but is not rich toward God."*

29

Rich Man and Lazarus

Luke 16:19-31 (NLT): *Jesus said, "There was a certain rich man who was splendidly clothed in purple and fine linen and who lived each day in luxury. At his gate lay a poor man named Lazarus who was covered with sores. As Lazarus lay there longing for scraps from the rich man's table, the dogs would come and lick his open sores. Finally, the poor man died and was carried by the angels to sit beside Abraham at the heavenly banquet. The rich man also died and was buried, and he went to the place of the dead. There, in torment, he saw Abraham in the far distance with Lazarus at his side.*

"The rich man shouted, 'Father Abraham, have some pity! Send Lazarus over here to dip the tip of his finger in water and cool my tongue. I am in anguish in these flames.' "But Abraham said to him, 'Son, remember that during your lifetime you had everything you wanted, and Lazarus had nothing. So now he is here being comforted, and you are in anguish. And besides, there is a great chasm separating us. No one can cross over to you from here, and no one can cross over to us from there.' "Then the rich man said, 'Please, Father Abraham, at least send him to my father's home. For I

have five brothers, and I want him to warn them so they don't end up in this place of torment.' But Abraham said, 'Moses and the prophets have warned them. Your brothers can read what they wrote.'

"The rich man replied, 'No, Father Abraham! But if someone is sent to them from the dead, then they will repent of their sins and turn to God.' But Abraham said, 'If they won't listen to Moses and the prophets, they won't be persuaded even if someone rises from the dead.'"

30

Savor of Salt

Luke 14:34-35 (NLT): *"Salt is good for seasoning. But if it loses its flavor, how do you make it salty again? Flavorless salt is good neither for the soil nor for the manure pile. It is thrown away. Anyone with ears to hear should listen and understand!"*

31
Sheep and Goats

Matthew 25:31-46 (NLT): *"But when the Son of Man comes in his glory, and all the angels with him, then he will sit upon his glorious throne. All the nations will be gathered in his presence, and he will separate the people as a shepherd separates the sheep from the goats. He will place the sheep at his right hand and the goats at his left.*

"Then the King will say to those on his right, 'Come, you who are blessed by my Father, inherit the Kingdom prepared for you from the creation of the world. For I was hungry, and you fed me. I was thirsty, and you gave me a drink. I was a stranger, and you invited me into your home. 36 I was naked, and you gave me clothing. I was sick, and you cared for me. I was in prison, and you visited me.'

"Then these righteous ones will reply, 'Lord, when did we ever see you hungry and feed you? Or thirsty and give you something to drink? Or a stranger and show you hospitality? Or naked and give you clothing? When did we ever see you sick or in prison and visit you?' And the King will say, 'I tell you the truth, when you did it to one of the least of these my brothers and sisters, you were doing it to me!'

"Then the King will turn to those on the left and say, 'Away with you, you cursed ones, into the eternal fire prepared for the devil and his demons. For I was hungry, and you didn't feed me. I was thirsty, and you didn't give me a drink. I was a stranger, and you didn't invite me into your home. I was naked, and you didn't give me clothing. I was sick and in prison, and you didn't visit me.' Then they will reply, 'Lord, when did we ever see you hungry or thirsty or a stranger or naked or sick or in prison, and not help you?'

"And he will answer, 'I tell you the truth, when you refused to help the least of these my brothers and sisters, you were refusing to help me.' And they will go away into eternal punishment, but the righteous will go into eternal life."

32
Shrewd Manager

Luke 16:1-13 (NIV): *Jesus told his disciples: "There was a rich man whose manager was accused of wasting his possessions. So he called him in and asked him, 'What is this I hear about you? Give an account of your management, because you cannot be manager any longer.' The manager said to himself, 'What shall I do now? My master is taking away my job. I'm not strong enough to dig, and I'm ashamed to beg—I know what I'll do so that, when I lose my job here, people will welcome me into their houses.' So he called in each one of his master's debtors. He asked the first, 'How much do you owe my master?' 'Nine hundred gallons of olive oil,' he replied. The manager told him, 'Take your bill, sit down quickly, and make it four hundred and fifty.'*

Then he asked the second, 'And how much do you owe?' 'A thousand bushels of wheat,' he replied. He told him, 'Take your bill and make it eight hundred.' The master commended the dishonest manager because he had acted shrewdly. For the people of this world are more shrewd in dealing with their own kind than are the people of the light. I tell you, use worldly wealth to gain friends for yourselves, so that when it is gone, you will be welcomed into eternal dwellings. Whoever can be trusted with very little can also be trusted with much, and whoever is dishonest with very little will also be dishonest with much. So if you have not been trustworthy in handling worldly wealth, who will trust you with true riches? And if you have not been trustworthy with someone else's property, who will give you property of your own? No one can serve two masters. Either you will hate the one and love the other, or you will be devoted to the one and despise the other. You cannot serve both God and money."

33
Sower and the Seeds

Matthew 13:3-8, 18-23 (NKJV): *Then He spoke many things to them in parables, saying: "Behold, a sower went out to sow. And as he sowed, some seed fell by the wayside; and the birds came and devoured them. Some fell on stony places, where they did not have much earth; and they immediately sprang up because they had no depth of earth. But when the sun was up they were scorched, and because they had no root they withered away. And some fell among thorns, and the thorns sprang up and choked them. But others fell on good ground and yielded a crop: some a hundredfold, some sixty, some thirty. …Therefore hear the parable of the sower: When anyone hears the word of the kingdom, and does not understand it, then the wicked one comes and snatches away what was sown in his heart. This is he who received seed by the wayside. But he who received the seed on stony places, this is he who hears the word and immediately receives it with joy; yet he has no root in himself, but endures only for a while. For when tribulation or persecution arises because of the word, immediately he stumbles. Now he who received seed among the thorns is he who hears the word, and the cares of this world and the deceitfulness of riches choke the word, and he becomes unfruitful. But he who received seed on the good ground is he who hears the word and understands it, who indeed bears fruit and produces: some a hundredfold, some sixty, some thirty."* (See also Mark 4:3-8, 13-20; Luke 8:5-8, 11-15.)

34

Speck and the Log

Luke 6:41-42 (NLT): *"And why worry about a speck in your friend's eye when you have a log in your own? How can you think of saying, 'Friend, let me help you get rid of that speck in your eye,' when you can't see past the log in your own eye? Hypocrite! First get rid of the log in your own eye; then you will see well enough to deal with the speck in your friend's eye."*

35

Strong Man Armed

Mark 3:27 (NLT): *"Let me illustrate this further. Who is powerful enough to enter the house of a strong man and plunder his goods? Only someone even stronger— someone who could tie him up and then plunder his house."* (See also Luke 11:21.)

36
Ten Bridesmaids

Matthew 25:1-13 (NKJV): *"Then the kingdom of heaven shall be likened to ten virgins who took their lamps and went out to meet the bridegroom. Now five of them were wise, and five were foolish. Those who were foolish took their lamps and took no oil with them, but the wise took oil in their vessels with their lamps. But while the bridegroom was delayed, they all slumbered and slept. And at midnight a cry was heard: 'Behold, the bridegroom is coming; go out to meet him!' Then all those virgins arose and trimmed their lamps. And the foolish said to the wise, 'Give us some of your oil, for our lamps are going out.' But the wise answered, saying, 'No, lest there should not be enough for us and you; but go rather to those who sell, and buy for yourselves.' And while they went to buy, the bridegroom came, and those who were ready went in with him to the wedding; and the door was shut. Afterward the other virgins came also, saying, 'Lord, Lord, open to us!' But he answered and said, 'Assuredly, I say to you, I do not know you.' Watch therefore, for you know neither the day nor the hour in which the Son of Man is coming."*

37
Ten Servants

Luke 19:11-26 (NLT): *The crowd was listening to everything Jesus said. And because he was nearing Jerusalem, he told them a story to correct the impression that the Kingdom of God would begin right away. He said, "A nobleman was called away to a distant empire to be crowned king and then return. Before he left, he called together ten of his servants and divided among them ten pounds of silver, saying, 'Invest this for me while I am gone.' But his people hated him and sent a delegation after him to say, 'We do not want him to be our king.' After he was crowned king, he returned and called in the servants to whom he had given the money. He wanted to find out what their profits were. The first servant reported, 'Master, I invested your money and made ten times the original amount!' 'Well done!' the king exclaimed. 'You are a good servant. You have been faithful with the little I entrusted to you, so you will be governor of ten cities as your reward.' The next servant reported, 'Master, I invested your money and made five times the original amount.' 'Well done!' the king said. 'You will be governor over five cities.' But the third servant brought back only the original amount of money and said, 'Master, I hid your money and kept it safe. I was afraid because you are a hard man to deal with, taking what isn't yours and harvesting crops you didn't plant.' 'You wicked servant!' the king roared. 'Your own words condemn you. If you knew that I'm a hard man who takes what isn't mine and harvests crops I didn't plant, why didn't you deposit my money in the bank? At least I could have gotten some interest on it.' Then, turning to the others standing nearby, the king ordered, 'Take the money from this servant, and give it to the one who has ten pounds.' 'But, master,' they said, 'he already has ten pounds!' 'Yes,' the king replied, 'and to those who use well what they are given, even more will be given. But from those who do nothing, even what little they have will be taken away.*

38

The Invitation

John 3:16 (NKJV): *"For God so loved the world, that He gave His only begotten Son, that whoever believes in Him should not perish but have everlasting life."*

39

Tree and its Fruit

Luke 6:43-45 (NLT): *"A good tree can't produce bad fruit, and a bad tree can't produce good fruit. A tree is identified by its fruit. Figs are never gathered from thornbushes, and grapes are not picked from bramble bushes. A good person produces good things from the treasury of a good heart, and an evil person produces evil things from the treasury of an evil heart. What you say flows from what is in your heart."*

40

Two Sons

Matthew 21:28-32 (NIV): *"What do you think? There was a man who had two sons. He went to the first and said, 'Son, go and work today in the vineyard.' 'I will not,' he answered, but later he changed his mind and went. Then the father went to the other son and said the same thing. He answered, 'I will, sir,' but he did not go. Which of the two did what his father wanted?" "The first," they answered. Jesus said to them, "Truly I tell you, the tax collectors and the prostitutes are entering the kingdom of God ahead of you. For John came to you to show you the way of righteousness, and you did not believe him, but the tax collectors and the prostitutes did. And even after you saw this, you did not repent and believe him."*

_____

_____

_____

_____

41

Unclean Spirit

Matthew 12:43 (NIV): *"When an impure spirit comes out of a person, it goes through arid places seeking rest and does not find it."*

42

Unfruitful Fig Tree

Luke 13:6-9 (NIV): *Then he told this parable: "A man had a fig tree growing in his vineyard, and he went to look for fruit on it but did not find any. So he said to the man who took care of the vineyard, 'For three years now I've been coming to look for fruit on this fig tree and haven't found any. Cut it down! Why should it use up the soil?' 'Sir,' the man replied, 'leave it alone for one more year, and I'll dig around it and fertilize it. If it bears fruit next year, fine! If not, then cut it down.'"*

43
Unmerciful Servant

Matthew 18:23-35 (NIV): *"Therefore, the kingdom of heaven is like a king who wanted to settle accounts with his servants. As he began the settlement, a man who owed him ten thousand bags of gold was brought to him. Since he was not able to pay, the master ordered that he and his wife and his children and all that he had be sold to repay the debt. At this the servant fell on his knees before him. 'Be patient with me,' he begged, 'and I will pay back everything.' The servant's master took pity on him, canceled the debt and let him go. But when that servant went out, he found one of his fellow servants who owed him a hundred silver coins. He grabbed him and began to choke him. 'Pay back what you owe me!' he demanded. His fellow servant fell to his knees and begged him, 'Be patient with me, and I will pay it back.' But he refused. Instead, he went off and had the man thrown into prison until he could pay the debt. When the other servants saw what had happened, they were outraged and went and told their master everything that had happened. Then the master called the servant in. 'You wicked servant,' he said, 'I canceled all that debt of yours because you begged me to. Shouldn't you have had mercy on your fellow servant just as I had on you?' In anger his master handed him over to the jailers to be tortured, until he should pay back all he owed. This is how my heavenly Father will treat each of you unless you forgive your brother or sister from your heart."*

44

Valuable Pearl

Matthew 13:45-46 (NLT): *"Again, the Kingdom of Heaven is like a merchant on the lookout for choice pearls. When he discovered a pearl of great value, he sold everything he owned and bought it!"*

45

Vine and the Branches

John 15:1-5 (NLT): *"I am the true grapevine, and my Father is the gardener. He cuts off every branch of mine that doesn't produce fruit, and he prunes the branches that do bear fruit so they will produce even more. You have already been pruned and purified by the message I have given you. Remain in me, and I will remain in you. For a branch cannot produce fruit if it is severed from the vine, and you cannot be fruitful unless you remain in me. Yes, I am the vine; you are the branches. Those who remain in me, and I in them, will produce much fruit. For apart from me you can do nothing."*

46

Vineyard Workers

Matthew 20:1-16 (NLT): *"For the Kingdom of Heaven is like the landowner who went out early one morning to hire workers for his vineyard. He agreed to pay the normal daily wage and sent them out to work. At nine o'clock in the morning he was passing through the marketplace and saw some people standing around doing nothing. So he hired them, telling them he would pay them whatever was right at the end of the day. So they went to work in the vineyard. At noon and again at three o'clock he did the same thing. At five o'clock that afternoon he was in town again and saw some more people standing around. He asked them, 'Why haven't you been working today?' They replied, 'Because no one hired us.' The landowner told them, 'Then go out and join the others in my vineyard.' That evening he told the foreman to call the workers in and pay them, beginning with the last workers first. When those hired at five o'clock were paid, each received a full day's wage. When those hired first came to get their pay, they assumed they would receive more. But they, too, were paid a day's wage. When they received their pay, they protested to the owner, 'Those people worked only one hour, and yet you've paid them just as much as you paid us who worked all day in the scorching heat.' He answered one of them, 'Friend, I haven't been unfair! Didn't you agree to work all day for the usual wage? Take your money and go. I wanted to pay this last worker the same as you. Is it against the law for me to do what I want with my money? Should you be jealous because I am kind to others?' So those who are last now will be first then, and those who are first will be last."*

47

Watchful Homeowner

Matthew 24:43 (NIV): *"But understand this: If the owner of the house had known at what time of night the thief was coming, he would have kept watch and would not have let his house be broken into."*

48

Watchful Servants

Mark 13:32-37 (NKJV): *"But of that day and hour no one knows, not even the angels in heaven, nor the Son, but only the Father. Take heed, watch and pray; for you do not know when the time is. It is like a man going to a far country, who left his house and gave authority to his servants, and to each his work, and commanded the doorkeeper to watch. Watch therefore, for you do not know when the master of the house is coming—in the evening, at midnight, at the crowing of the rooster, or in the morning—lest, coming suddenly, he find you sleeping. And what I say to you, I say to all: Watch!"* (See also Luke 12:35-40.)

49
Wedding Banquet

Matthew 22:2-14 (NKJV): *"The kingdom of heaven is like a certain king who arranged a marriage for his son, and sent out his servants to call those who were invited to the wedding; and they were not willing to come. Again, he sent out other servants, saying, 'Tell those who are invited, "See, I have prepared my dinner; my oxen and fatted cattle are killed, and all things are ready. Come to the wedding."' But they made light of it and went their ways, one to his own farm, another to his business. And the rest seized his servants, treated them spitefully, and killed them. But when the king heard about it, he was furious. And he sent out his armies, destroyed those murderers, and burned up their city. Then he said to his servants, 'The wedding is ready, but those who were invited were not worthy. Therefore go into the highways, and as many as you find, invite to the wedding.' So those servants went out into the highways and gathered together all whom they found, both bad and good. And the wedding hall was filled with guests. But when the king came in to see the guests, he saw a man there who did not have on a wedding garment. So he said to him, 'Friend, how did you come in here without a wedding garment?' And he was speechless. Then the king said to the servants, 'Bind him hand and foot, take him away, and cast him into outer darkness; there will be weeping and gnashing of teeth.' For many are called, but few are chosen."* (Also see Luke 14:16-24.)

50
Weeds in the Field

Matthew 13:24-30, 36-43 (NKJV): *Another parable He put forth to them, saying: "The kingdom of heaven is like a man who sowed good seed in his field; but while men slept, his enemy came and sowed tares among the wheat and went his way. But when the grain had sprouted and produced a crop, then the tares also appeared. So the servants of the owner came and said to him, 'Sir, did you not sow good seed in your field? How then does it have tares?' He said to them, 'An enemy has done this.' The servants said to him, 'Do you want us then to go and gather them up?' But he said, 'No, lest while you gather up the tares you also uproot the wheat with them. Let both grow together until the harvest, and at the time of harvest I will say to the reapers, "First gather together the tares and bind them in bundles to burn them, but gather the wheat into my barn."'" ...Then Jesus sent the multitude away and went into the house. And His disciples came to Him, saying, "Explain to us the parable of the tares of the field." He answered and said to them: "He who sows the good seed is the Son of Man. The field is the world, the good seeds are the sons of the kingdom, but the tares are the sons of the wicked one. The enemy who sowed them is the devil, the harvest is the end of the age, and the reapers are the angels. Therefore as the tares are gathered and burned in the fire, so it will be at the end of this age. The Son of Man will send out His angels, and they will gather out of His kingdom all things that offend, and those who practice lawlessness, and will cast them into the furnace of fire. There will be wailing and gnashing of teeth. Then the righteous will shine forth as the sun in the kingdom of their Father. He who has ears to hear, let him hear!"*

51

Wise and Foolish Builders

Matthew 7:24-27 (NLT): *"Anyone who listens to my teaching and follows it is wise, like a person who builds a house on solid rock. Though the rain comes in torrents and the floodwaters rise and the winds beat against that house, it won't collapse because it is built on bedrock. But anyone who hears my teaching and doesn't obey it is foolish, like a person who builds a house on sand. When the rains and floods come and the winds beat against that house, it will collapse with a mighty crash."* (See also Luke:46-49.)

52

Yeast

Matthew 13:33 (NIV): *He told them still another parable: "The kingdom of heaven is like yeast that a woman took and mixed into about sixty pounds of flour until it worked all through the dough."* (See also Luke 13:18-19.)

Conclusion
Revelation on Relationships and Life

Much of how you perceive the quality of your life is tied to your relationships. The better relationships you create, the better life you will enjoy. It's hard to believe it's that easy, but it's true—all positives in our relationships come from God and all negatives can be attributed to Satan.

Leveraging the synergy that *The Kingdom Network* can produce will accelerate the good in your relationships. Going outside the network for what appears to be a "success shortcut" will often turn out to be counterproductive and/or self-destructive.

God always wants us to succeed. He created *The Kingdom Network* so that we would have the tools and support needed for the success He has planned for us all along. And then He sent Jesus to show us how the network can be used, and the Holy Spirit to help us steer past the obstacles.

We pray that this book has brought you insight into The Kingdom Network and that you will choose to be an active member of this networking group of like-minded Christians. Based on God's Word and specifically the parables Jesus shared with His disciples and others, the wisdom and scenarios are sure to mend, expand, and enhance all your relationships—at home, work, church, and in every endeavor.

Welcome to *The Kingdom Network*—let's grow it together!

www.ingramcontent.com/pod-product-compliance
Lightning Source LLC
Chambersburg PA
CBHW030334100526
44592CB00010B/700